A JOURNAL OF PRAYER AND REFLECTION

GW00729004

EMOTIONAL
WISDOM

ROBERT MACLENNAN

Augsburg Books
MINNEAPOLIS

to Douglas Tindal
for enabling a context
for the writing of this book

EMOTIONAL WISDOM
A Journal of Prayer and Reflection

Large-quantity purchases or custom editions of this book are available
at a discount from the publisher. For more information,
contact the sales department at Augsburg Fortress, Publishers,
P.O. Box 1209, Minneapolis, MN 55440-1209.

Unless otherwise indicated, Scripture quotations are from the
New Revised Standard Version Bible, copyright © 1989
by the Division of Christian Education of the National Council
of the Churches of Christ in the USA and used by permission.

Cover design by Dave Meyer
Cover photo © Taxi/Getty Images. Used by permission.
Book design by Michelle L. N. Cook

ISBN 0-8066-5140-7

The paper used in this publication meets the minimum requirements
of American National Standard for Information Sciences—
Permanence of Paper for Printed Library Materials, ANSI Z329.48-1985. ∞ ™

Manufactured in the U.S.A.

09 08 07 06   05 1 2 3 4 5 6 7 8 9 10

CONTENTS

EXPLORING INNER AND OUTER NATURE

You may have decided to begin, or to continue, the rewarding process of exploring your inner life and living in harmony with your outer world. This book is a tool for such personal discovery and development. It is only one of many similar resources, and it is flexible. You may want to use it as it is presented, or you may prefer to adapt it to suit your current needs. Later in this introduction, there are some suggestions for different ways of using this book.

Emotions are the spice of life. This book is intended to help you to get in touch with your emotions and the natural world—the inner and outer realities that urgently need to be understood and appreciated more deeply today. Our feelings profoundly influence our thoughts and actions, and have tremendous impact on our lives, the lives of others, and the world around us. Similarly, the natural environment impinges not only on our physical health and safety, but also on our emotional and spiritual well-being. Most people have experienced, for example, how much the weather affects their moods.

If we do not learn to work with emotion and nature, they can work against us. When we suppress anger or love, they can leak out, and may no longer express what we originally intended. When we pillage the earth and poison the water and air, they can "fight back," and may no longer support life as we know it. When we suppress emotions associated with unpleasant memories, we can blunt our ability to feel anything, even good times, and our life and our world begin to lose their luster. By nurturing our relationship with human feeling and the natural environment, we can renew and deepen our connection with the Power that creates and sustains us and all life.

The Bible is a wonderful resource to spark our exploration of inner and outer nature. Many biblical stories evoke powerful feelings, and some biblical writers portray intimate connections among divinity, humanity, and nature. The Bible's wisdom literature—including such books as Proverbs, Psalms, and Ecclesiastes—and the gospel accounts of Jesus's words, provide many insights to help us engage our emotions. The biblical passages included in *Emotional Wisdom* draw from these ancient texts as well from other books of the Old and New Testaments.

Your own experience is a precious source of wisdom and guidance. Over many years, my experience has been my teacher and is my primary source for writing this book. The important thing, of course, is not necessarily to agree with my thoughts or to duplicate my experiences but, through thinking and feeling about your own emotions, to become more aware of them, to understand them better, and, above all, to appreciate them. I hope that this book will become a helpful companion on your path to emotional wisdom and enjoyment.

The material provided on the following pages can be part of a weekly or daily routine of reading and reflection. There are enough topics in this book for forty-four weeks of the year—the remaining weeks can be well-deserved time off! Or the meditations can be compressed into a shorter time, such as forty-four days—there is no special significance to forty-four. The topics are arranged in alphabetical order for easy reference.

Not all the topics in this book are always thought of as emotions, although most include emotional content. Conversely, some emotions you are familiar with may not be mentioned here, and you might decide to add these emotions to your meditation schedule.

You may decide to work through the topics from beginning to end, devise another order in advance, or select topics as you go, according to circumstance. You can always repeat a topic any time. Although you may select a sequence of topics, give yourself freedom to change. Our emotions don't work to a schedule! But in this kind of spiritual work, establishing a plan and being regular in your practice are important.

For each week or day, a particular emotion—such as awe, joy, pain—is the subject of exploration. A biblical quotation and reflection start each meditation. Following the reflection are questions or suggestions of things to think about and feel, and space for making notes. If you use this book once a week, you can use this space to note the ideas that you plan to consider throughout the week. You might also use the space at the top of each journal page or the table of contents to record the date when you have worked on a topic, so that you will have a record of what you have done.

In your plan for using this material, include details of time and place. Select a time of day when you can be undisturbed. It may be first thing in the morning or last thing at night. It may be after breakfast when everyone else is gone or during lunch when you can close a door or find a quiet place away from work. Take at least ten minutes if possible, or at most twenty minutes.

Ideally, use the same space each time you meditate. It should be quiet, clean, and orderly because your mind can be influenced by the condition of your physical surroundings. Find a place to sit comfortably with sufficient light to read and write, not too bright. It is also important, when doing any concentrated inner work, to make sure that the body is comfortable and relaxed, so that feelings and thoughts can range freely. Here are three things to try:

- Find a comfortable position, neither slouching nor rigid, so that your body sits with ease; no limb is pressured, and no muscles are unduly tensed.
- Pay attention to your breathing for a minute or two, following the out-breath and the in-breath, waiting until a reasonable degree of calm and regularity is achieved.
- Relax all of your body, from toe to head or from head to toe. For example, feel your feet, calves, thighs, abdomen, chest, hands, lower arms, upper arms, back, shoulders, neck, face, head.

Here is a possible meditation plan. On the first day with a topic, read the biblical quotation and the reflection. Think about how they compare with your ideas and experiences of the emotion. Do you agree? Disagree? Would you add anything? Subtract anything? Briefly note your thoughts and feelings in the space provided. If there is not enough space on the page, you may want to keep your own notebook.

Next, plan the coming week. If you have not already set your schedule, decide which day, or days, you will do this work, what time, and what place. Again, whatever schedule you plan, be regular. Next, plan your agenda for the "inner work." First, you could ponder key words in the biblical quotation. Second, you might resonate with an idea in the reflection. Third, you could consider some of the questions and suggestions. Fourth, you could supply your own agenda for emotional exploration.

On the next day or days, begin with the same procedure that you used for the first day—when, where, how. After you have relaxed, recall the topic you have chosen for the day, and hold it *gently* in your mind and heart. Almost casually, consider what you think of it and how you feel about it. Your thoughts and feelings may wander, but don't let this bother you. Human awareness is normally, and constantly, on the move. When you realize that you have wandered, simply observe where you are. Have you arrived anywhere interesting or useful? If so, make a brief note of it on the page or in your notebook. Then *gently* bring yourself back to the topic and start again.

It is possible that you may find yourself recalling something painful. Above all, do not blame yourself for this. Instead, thank yourself for letting you feel again. Acknowledge the pain. Give it your understanding and comfort. You deserve, as much as anyone living, to be loved and healed of pain. It is also possible that you may remember something joyful. Savor the feeling.

When it seems that this work is finished for the day (between ten and twenty minutes from starting), thank yourself and the God of the universe for the time and the ideas, bring yourself back to full waking consciousness (perhaps by clapping your hands or stamping your feet), and make any final notes. The session is not complete until you have cemented your ideas in writing. Some day you may want to review your work.

Enjoy!

ANGER

Those with good sense are slow to anger,
and it is their glory to overlook an offense.
Proverbs 19:11

Anger is an honest emotion. If we bury anger, it can vent when least expected, with surprising force and damaging results. If we govern anger, our response can often be expressed appropriately and constructively.

When someone assaults us with anger, we can try to delay our natural reaction and ask ourselves some questions. Was it meant to hurt? If so, the other person might have a problem, not us. We may consider, by our response, how we could help the person to get hold of their emotion. Was it meant to correct? If so, we may have been at fault, but the other person might have behaved inappropriately. We may be grateful for correction, but the mode of expression might need adjustment too.

When we or society have been wronged, anger may seem justified. But again we need to pause. An angry response can create more anger and perpetuate the problem. How can we react beneficially? With a friend or colleague, we can meet and find a reasonable resolution. With a government or corporation, we can use or build productive communication channels—worker associations or advocacy groups, print or electronic media. In this way our anger can be transformed and put to work for ourselves, our society, and our environment.

Like an electrical storm, anger can inflict irreparable damage. But it can also "clear the air." Storm clouds gather and lightning cleaves the sky. Thunder crashes and rain pelts down. The elements rage. But after the storm, the air is cleansed, the water replenished, and the earth refreshed. New life will surely follow.

~ *Think of a time when you have vented your anger.*
~ *How could you have responded more constructively?*
~ *Think of a time when you have felt another's anger.*
~ *How could you have helped to resolve the situation?*
~ *Compose a prayer for help with anger, yours or another's.*

_____

_____

_____

_____

_____

_____

_____

_____

_____

_____

_____

_____

_____

_____

AWE

The fear of the LORD
is the beginning of wisdom.
Psalm 111:10

We see, hear, smell, taste, and touch. Our five senses give us impressions of the world around and within us. The results can be pleasing or offensive. Sometimes we receive impressions beyond the normal scope of our senses. Such experiences can fill us with awe.

An impression of awe can seem both blissful and fearful. It is strangely exhilarating, agreeably disturbing, and outside the normal. No wonder we associate awe with an experience of the divine. Awe gives us a deeper awareness of the immediate presence of God.

We all remember occasions when we have touched, and been touched by, God. An encounter with divinity immeasurably enriches all life. We feel the wonder of a birth, see the beauty of a living being, or know the ecstasy of love. Such moments may indeed be rare, but their influence lasts a lifetime.

The experience of awe adds immeasurable richness to our life. Suddenly the world seems tinged with gold. Ourselves, people we know, things we experience—all gain a higher, broader, and deeper meaning. Our souls are cleansed and refreshed. We are filled with inexplicable happiness. This is not surprising, since we have just met a Friend who is kindest and wisest—closer and greater than the atom and the universe.

The divine dwells within and beyond all existence—in the nearest atom and the farthest star; in a tiny seed and a great forest; in the water droplet on a rose petal and the grain of sand on a mountaintop. The creating and sustaining energy of the Holy One permeates all things. We need only to perceive it!

~ *Recall a special experience of awe.*
~ *Relive your feelings of this experience.*
~ *What do they tell about the nature of God?*
~ *Could you share your discovery with a friend?*
~ *Offer a prayer of appreciation for the experience.*

COMPASSION

Clothe yourselves with compassion . . .
Bear with one another.
Colossians 3:12, 13

The sight of suffering can move us to compassion. Yet the more we empathize with those who suffer, the more suffering we seem to see and, in turn, the more compassion we need. Suffering is a condition of our physical existence. Earthly matter cannot fully express divine spirit. Our souls, too, long for an ideal that we cannot quite realize—the image of God within us—and as a result we suffer.

When pain dominates our awareness, joy departs. We may feel abandoned by the spirit and oppressed in matter. Life is no longer a journey in light, but a detour in shadow. Then compassion is needed—for both ourselves and others—to kindle a flame in darkness, to fortify spirit in flesh.

In a competitive society like ours, compassion seems a weakness. But compassion is really a spiritual strength. When hearts are linked in humane concern, the spirit of God flows freely, bringing health to each soul. A person who has received compassion tends to show compassion, and blessing grows in the world.

The New Testament letter of James affirms that God is "compassionate" (5:11). All the gospel stories depict the Son of God healing the sick, feeding the hungry, giving sight to the blind. And so, when we show compassion, we clothe ourselves in the very spirit of God, and serve to extend divine grace in the world.

All nature joins in suffering. Earth heaves and settles; plants grow and perish; animals strive and rest. The earth and all its creatures know both stress and pain. But God's gift of compassion, flowing through our divine humanity, can bring healing peace and joy.

~ *Think of some aspect of suffering in your life.*
~ *Let the spirit of God bring healing to the situation.*
~ *Offer a silent prayer of compassion for your suffering.*
~ *Repeat the above for someone or something else who suffers.*
~ *Offer a silent prayer of compassion for all of nature.*

CONFIDENCE

*The Lord will be your confidence
and will keep your foot from being caught.*
Proverbs 3:26

Confidence is developed by being realistic in our expectations and by striving to do the possible, not the impossible. If we start with goals that are challenging but within our power, we can reasonably expect to achieve them. We will then be practicing the art of confidence building. The future will offer plenty of opportunity to extend our efforts to more demanding goals.

Many people believe that spirituality should be concerned only with "higher" things, such as morality, good works, and spiritual development. But spiritual practice can help us to deal with mundane things as well. To mature in spirit, we need also to develop our creative powers responsibly in the context of physical existence. Our relationships and careers, entertainments and studies, can become productive resources for our confidence.

In every endeavor, our confidence can be reinforced if we invite spiritual assistance. Jesus said, "Whatever you ask for in prayer, believe that you have received it, and it will be yours" (Mark 11:24). When we turn toward God in expectant prayer, we open ourselves to the creative energy of the universe. As we gain experience in asking and receiving, we will learn to trust divine power and guidance, and our confidence will surely build.

When a fledgling sparrow first attempts to fly, it springs boldly from the nest but may only tumble to the ground, saved from disaster by a feeble flutter of wings. But it will recover. Having often seen its parents fly and once felt the air beneath its wings, it has gained a latent confidence that will soon lift it to exhilarating heights.

~ *Where does your greatest confidence lie?*
~ *What are you least confident about achieving?*
~ *Separate this goal into achievable stages.*
~ *Formulate a prayer for trust and help.*
~ *Consider helping someone build confidence.*

CONTEMPT

When wickedness comes, contempt comes also;
and with dishonor comes disgrace.
Proverbs 18:3

When others hold us in contempt, we need to remember that we are of value. Each one of us is a unique creation with a special purpose on earth. But we can appreciate the insecurity of those who condemn us. Their criticism seems to set them above others, and helps to bolster their self-esteem.

When a person treats us with contempt, we can ask ourselves what, if any, criticism may actually apply. We can also ask ourselves what motivation may drive such a person. By understanding them and ourselves more clearly, we can dissolve our self-pity and blame. We may even be able to help them achieve a more realistic picture of themselves and the world around them.

On the other hand, when we feel contempt for others, we need to ask ourselves whether they really deserve censure or help, or both. We need also to test what our own motives may be. Do we need to criticize others to boost our self-image, or are we really concerned to promote their self-awareness and self-development?

We could do much good in the world by promoting kind and generous behavior, instead of condemning. We need not wink at wickedness; we must resist inhumanity whenever we meet it. But we can also work for change and seek the value in all life.

What earthly creatures could be humbler than the earthworms? Yet their lowly state conceals an inestimable value. They help to aerate and drain the soil. They promote the growth of plants by dragging seeds into the ground and by opening passages for the roots.

~ *Determine why you have been criticized.*
~ *Determine why you have criticized another.*
~ *Ask God to help you understand clearly.*
~ *How could you improve the circumstances?*
~ *Pray that all may appreciate the value of life.*

CONTENTMENT

*There is great gain in godliness
combined with contentment.*
1 Timothy 6:6

Many people view contentment as a reward for acquiring enough of this world's goods, or achieving success in this world's goals—family and friends, car and house, degree and career, travel and leisure. But by these standards, other people would not judge themselves successful. How then can they find contentment?

There are deeper and more lasting criteria for contentment. Are there people who respect you for who you are, instead of what you have? They admire your kindness, loyalty, generosity. Are there friends who have watched you grow as a person? They know you have endured through stress, grief, illness.

When you look back on your life, have you not acquired invaluable possessions and achievements in the humanity you have shown, the maturity you have attained? You have indeed gained tremendously in knowledge and experience since you entered this world.

In the school of life, you have formed trusting relationships and learned rewarding lessons. In the process, you have acquired more character and wisdom—worthy riches and successes! Jesus, the great teacher, demonstrated that true humanity is an expression of true godliness. As we extend the best of ourselves to others, we also express the image of God in the world—an achievement worthy of contentment!

Leaves provide photosynthesis. Branches support leaves and conduct nourishment. Roots gather minerals and moisture, and anchor the plant. Flowers, fruit, and seeds ensure perpetuation. Each part fulfills its life by contributing to the life of the whole.

~ *List the challenges you have negotiated.*
~ *List the kindnesses you have shown to others.*
~ *Ask God to let you know contentment.*
~ *Consider someone who is very self-critical.*
~ *Pray that they may find contentment.*

COURAGE

Be strong and courageous;
do not be frightened or dismayed,
*for the L*ORD *your God is with you.*
Joshua 1:9

Many things can bear down on us, press against us, and even seem to crush us. They often appear to come in bunches. Some are serious—a severe illness, a lost position, a difficult child, a troubled relationship. Some seem serious but are less so—a relentless deadline, a broken promise, a harsh word.

In difficult circumstances, we all have inner resources to draw on. First, our memories. We have been in similar situations before, and we have won through. Then, other people. However hard we are pressed, we know there are others bearing more than we will ever have to. Also, our friends. It is never a weakness to share a problem with someone we trust. And ultimately our God. The strength and courage to win through adversity dwell all around us and within us. And we can reach for it!

We can also plan our way forward. We can take the initiative and turn things around. Exercising our creative faculties will give us courage. When we plan, all the support we have sought and gained is put to use, restoring our energy and shaping our life for good.

I have a friend who knows the meaning of courage. The stripes on his back have healed crookedly since a vicious attack by a predator. One ear was badly chewed during a scrap with a peer over territorial rights. His tail is now half its original length. But he is a valiant chipmunk. Nothing seems to deter him. Day after day he keeps up the earnest business of storing his larder with good seeds for the future.

~ *Consider a problem to solve.*
~ *Consult with someone you trust.*
~ *Ask God to show you a way forward.*
~ *Work out a constructive plan of action.*
~ *Say a prayer for someone who suffers.*

_____

_____

_____

_____

_____

_____

_____

_____

_____

_____

_____

_____

_____

_____

_____

DELIGHT

Take delight in the Lord,
and he will give you the desires of your heart.
Psalm 37:4

Too often the responsibilities of life leave us little time for delight. We must hold down a job, care for a family, manage our finances, look after the children, the sick, the elderly. The obligations seem overwhelming. We work hard at living.

We also feel the need to work hard at playing. We must keep healthy by getting exercise, live it up by joining the party, give ourselves a break by getting away. We can have lots of fun, but end up being as exhausted as ever. And we may reap very little delight.

When such destructive levels of activity ensnare us, we need to halt the frenzy and examine our lives. How can we break the cycle? If we slow down and look deeper, if we cut through the excess to expose the essential, we can consider, and maybe savor, our own experience. We may be surprised by delight.

Was there an exchange of anecdotes in an office corridor and a moment of sympathy? Was there a meeting that went well and a feeling of accomplishment? On stepping outside, did a refreshing wind brush the skin and bring a thrill of exhilaration? On lifting the phone, did a familiar voice touch the heart and bring comfort or happiness?

At the heart of its vast complexity lies the elegant simplicity of nature. A spider web glistening in the sun, a tinted leaf floating on a pond, a tender blossom nodding in the wind. We watch the colors and patterns; we feel the stillness and movement. And suddenly, mysteriously, we are at one with the grace behind the beauty. And our hearts are filled with delight.

~ *Reflect on some frenetic activity in your life.*
~ *Can you find a special moment in the frenzy?*
~ *Ask God to let you know delight in the moment.*
~ *Offer a prayer of appreciation for finding the delight.*
~ *Help someone else to find delight in a special moment.*

DESIRE

What the wicked dread will come upon them,
but the desire of the righteous will be granted.
Proverbs 10:24

Desire, or attraction, is the driving force of life. A beneficial desire develops our character and, by extension, helps others and all life. An inappropriate desire harms others and, by reflection, diminishes our own worthiness. But suppressing inappropriate desire can render us bitter and unfulfilled. What can we do with such desire?

We can seek balance—reciprocity—between our own desire and the desires of others. We may want advancement. How, in the process, can we enhance the good of others? We may want possessions. How, through their acquisition, can we supply the need of others?

There are many kinds of desire. The body seeks, among other things, food and movement; the heart, beauty and relationship; the mind, thought and creativity; the spirit, meaning and fulfillment. We can endeavor to transform inappropriate desire into beneficial desire of a different kind.

Each living being embodies a life desire. We may spend many years discovering it, but when we find it, there is no mistake. When we pursue it, although the way may be arduous, our strength and confidence increase. We receive help from the Source of all desire. Ourselves, others, and the world benefit. We contribute to the balance of forces in the universe. And we enjoy fulfillment of the spirit.

The mutual attraction of the sun and the earth sustains the orbit of our planet. The force of gravity and the speed of the earth are perfectly balanced. Our planet neither hurtles to a fiery destruction in the sun, nor spins off on a tangent into outer space. A balance of forces sustains the life of the solar system.

~ *Is there a goal that you strongly desire?*
~ *How will it benefit you, others, the world?*
~ *Is there some goal that has been frustrated?*
~ *Ask God to help you reclaim the energy.*
~ *Pray for someone who lacks a life goal.*

DESPAIR

We are afflicted in every way, but not crushed;
perplexed, but not driven to despair.
2 Corinthians 4:8

When despair overwhelms us, life seems hopeless. There is no remedy, no escape. Light has left our lives.

Sadly, in our time, convincing reasons for despair abound. People are starved, oppressed, and killed. Nature is pillaged and degraded. Human values are eroded. Personal and family life are compromised. What can we do? How can we find relief from despair?

In his famous equation, $E=mc^2$ (energy equals the mass of an object times the speed of light squared), Albert Einstein bequeathed us a beautiful view of reality. Light and energy are bound up and hidden in matter. Strike a match, and the profound truth of this equation flames before us.

Divine light and energy dwell also at the core of our being. The biblical creation story tells us that we are made in the image of God. St. Paul asserts that Christ dwells within us. If the love, wisdom, and power of the Creator live in each of us, then at the deepest level of our being there can be no reason for despair. But how can we access and express this inner divinity?

Whatever in our life has brought deep happiness, contentment, or fulfillment may in fact spring from this creative well of divine spirit. If we can spend some time to recall such special experiences from our past, and perhaps open our hearts to opportunities for similar experiences in the future, we may find a lamp to light our path out of despair.

During the short, dark days of winter, when gray sky covers cold land and the nights are long, we despair of new beginnings. But as sure as spring follows winter and warmth scatters cold, a new spring and a new life will sprout and bloom for us.

~ *Is there some despair in your life?*
~ *If not, offer a prayer of thanksgiving.*
~ *If so, pray for help to find your inner light.*
~ *Does someone you know live in despair?*
~ *Pray that they may find inner light.*

DISTRESS

You have been a fortress for me
and a refuge in the day of my distress.
Psalm 59:16

Distress troubles all life. The competitiveness of economic globalization tyrannizes the workplace. The degradation of the natural environment threatens world health. The demands of society—family, friends, career—often exhaust us. Our own expectations and activities can cause us stress. We may be making excessive demands on ourselves and others, and feel that life is escaping our control.

How can we deal with such distress? We may need to temper our demands on ourselves with patience and gentleness. We may want to "branch out" and replenish our resources or broaden our horizons. But in the turmoil, we hesitate to tackle one more task. There is a simple but profound solution. We can offer our distress to God.

Whenever our life energy is drained beyond endurance, we can invite God to share the distress. We can permit ourselves to experience the entirety of our trouble, and also allow the divine presence to embrace our whole being. We can imagine God feeling our hurt, knowing our sorrow, living our distress.

And the wonder! When we let our being flow to God, the being of God flows also in us. We may feel distress, but we need not dwell in it. We can rest and revel, instead, in the divine energy embracing, sustaining, and healing all existence.

At the first threat of danger, a mother duck swims away, calling loudly to her young. They paddle and flutter after her. At the beginning of spring, there were more than a dozen ducklings; by the end of the summer, there may be two or three. But the extreme distress of the mother has given way to pride in her splendid young companions.

∽ *Does your behavior cause you distress?*
∽ *Does your environment cause you distress?*
∽ *Give your distress to the healing power of God.*
∽ *Do you know someone suffering from distress?*
∽ *Give their situation to the healing power of God.*

_____

_____

_____

_____

_____

_____

_____

_____

_____

_____

_____

_____

_____

_____

_____

_____

_____

DOUBT

Without any doubt,
the mystery of our religion is great.
1 Timothy 3:16

Doubt can be beneficial, prompting us to pause and analyze a motivation or situation. It can be detrimental, leading us to confusion, stagnation, or rash action. When in doubt, we need to consider all the known facts and our own observations, and to ponder them again and again. But finally, we need to consult our intuition.

Surprisingly, doubt can lead us to value our inner voice. This underused gift can convey wisdom from the realm where all the probabilities and consequences of our behavior are projected. There are many ways to nurture and access our intuition. Mostly we need to be encouraging and patient with ourselves, as if we were conversing with a diffident friend.

How do we feel when recalling something beneficial in our life, or something detrimental? Compare these "good" and "bad" feelings. Now, how do we feel when considering the subject of our doubt—good or bad? In this simple process, we are opening to our intuition, and discerning the wisdom of the soul.

Intuition takes time to develop. We need to practice listening to our inner self, and discriminating between true and false voices. The more we consult our intuition, the easier it is to hear and choose. Should we say "yes" or "no"? Should we speak or stay silent? Eventually, when in doubt, we will come to rely on our wise and trusted inner guide.

We study cloud formations, feel the movement of the air, note the quality of the light—deeply experiencing the world around us. As a result, we can forecast rain or sun. With practice, we can learn to read the soul of nature. And with practice, we can learn to weather our doubts!

~ *Is there a particular doubt that bothers you?*
~ *Have you gathered all the information you can?*
~ *Have you sought intuition concerning this doubt?*
~ *Pray for clarity and faithfulness of intuition.*
~ *Help someone in doubt to consult intuition.*

ENVY

Where there is envy and selfish ambition,
there will also be disorder and wickedness of every kind.
James 3:16

At every turn, we are pressured to spend more, get more, be more. Our consumer-driven culture assaults us with a dizzying barrage of images, telling us how we should act, what we should have, who we should be. If we find ourselves envying others, this is no surprise.

How can we respond? We can turn away from the exterior images and look at our own self-image. What are our gifts? How can we grow them? Who can help us? When we find our own center, we can begin to plan and act for ourselves, instead of imitating others.

We can also begin to acknowledge and appreciate ourselves. By recognizing our past achievements and acknowledging our present potential, we can equip ourselves for future accomplishments. Then the sting drops out of envy. A zest propels our efforts, and a poise governs our lives.

Each one of us is special. Our uniqueness derives from the infinite variety of creation. When we seek to develop our gifts, we draw on the abundance of our limitless source. There is no need for envy. No one can duplicate our gifts. We alone can offer our distinctive and inimitable contribution to the life of our world and the bounty of creation.

An ecosystem is a self-perpetuating, self-regulating organism. Each species is uniquely adapted to derive support *from* other species in the system (animal, vegetable, or mineral), and to provide support *for* other species. Each member of the ecosystem, fulfilling its life purpose, makes an essential and unique contribution to the life of the whole.

~ *Does something or someone arouse your envy?*
~ *How does this image link with your own true image?*
~ *What would you need to support and develop your image?*
~ *Ask God to help you discover those things you need.*
~ *Pray that others may lose envy and find their truth.*

FEAR

Fear is tremendously disabling. It can restrict both feeling and thought, inhibiting our ability to experience and respond to life. It can absorb all our attention, or it can hide from our awareness. When a negative emotion such as fear is suppressed, our ability to feel anything, pleasant or unpleasant, is reduced. As a result, life seems dull, and it takes more to move us. We find it harder to enjoy and adapt to life, to excel and be fulfilled.

But fear has its uses. It can alert us to potentially dangerous situations and people, or areas of our life that may need adjustment or healing. We need not blame ourselves for our fears. They are legitimate for us, no matter how inexplicable they may appear to others. But it is up to us to deal with them.

First, we need to identify our fears by noting things that affect us adversely. What makes us confused or frightened, or gives us discomfort—like butterflies in the stomach? Second, we need to discover the cause of our fears. Some former problem makes us sensitive? Some mistaken belief inhibits us? Some apparent obstacle threatens us? Third, we need to manage our fear. How can we change our attitude, our behavior, or our environment? Who can help or advise us in the situation? By effectively exercising our reason, we can begin to face and deal with our fears.

When an animal is frightened, it may run or hide. Then, after a period of caution, it investigates. It smells carefully, looks sharply, listens intently, and exercises judgment. When the threat has passed, the animal lets go of fear. It resumes life with zest and grace.

~ *Consider someone or something you fear.*
~ *Can you determine the true cause of your fear?*
~ *Ask God to help you find a remedy for the fear.*
~ *Pray for something or someone you may fear.*
~ *Offer prayer for someone who suffers fear.*

_____

_____

_____

_____

_____

_____

_____

_____

_____

_____

_____

_____

_____

_____

FREEDOM

The Lord is the Spirit,
and where the Spirit of the Lord is, there is freedom.
2 Corinthians 3:17

We can never be free of care or duty. But we can be free of domination by our concerns. Our attitude toward life and our skill in dealing with it, not escaping from it, contribute to our freedom. Emotions are signs, showing the results of our interaction with life. If we are ruled by our emotions, they become barriers that inhibit our experience of reality. If we enjoy their energy and employ their wisdom, we can gain freedom.

When we are afflicted by a "bad" emotion or intoxicated by a "good" one, we can work to transform our experience. We can consider the bad without trying to escape it by action or suppression. Then we are free to wrestle with it. Conversely, we can appreciate the good without attempting to retain it by control or possession. Then we are free to fly with it. Either way, we promote our own independence.

When we can open ourselves to the fullness of our emotions, even the "bad" ones, then we are liberated. We feel alive. The energy of the universe flows through us, and we experience the freedom of the spirit of God.

Because God is beyond and within all things, to open ourselves to the divine spirit is to connect with all existence. To know such freedom is neither to escape nor control. It is to delve into the deepest reality and to fly to the farthest star.

With a deft flick of the wing, a songbird darts from a slender branch to soar with speed and grace. Much lies behind this wonderful skill— learning to fly, finding food, avoiding predators, building nests, feeding young. The gift of freedom rests on responsibility.

~ *Recall an experience of strong emotion.*
~ *Rest in this memory without worry or fear.*
~ *Let the divine energy of spirit flow through you.*
~ *Offer a prayer of thanks for this experience of freedom.*
~ *Pray for someone who is ruled by their emotions.*

FRUSTRATION

The Lord is near to the brokenhearted,
and saves the crushed in spirit.
Psalm 34:18

Our frustrations can rouse sympathy for others who are frustrated. Our frustrations can also teach us about ourselves. We often blame people and circumstances for our difficulties. But instead of projecting the cause of our frustration outward, we might seek it in our own patterns of thought, feeling, and action.

In spite of our best efforts to the contrary, do we continually find ourselves in similar situations or with similar types of people? This is the sign of an unconscious pattern ruling our lives. We need not blame ourselves. Our patterns have evolved creatively to help us cope with the troubles of childhood and later years.

We have survived! But circumstances have now changed. Our defensive patterns may be hindering and not helping us, and we may want to change too. By getting a picture of our patterns and seeing how they rule us, we can begin to regain our autonomy.

A daily journal or a skillful counselor can act as a mirror to help us identify our patterns. Each day, we can recall and record significant things thought or felt, said or done. As we gradually bring our patterns to awareness, their formerly imprisoned energy will be released and their tyranny over us dissolved. In this way, by teaching us to acquire self-knowledge through self-examination, our frustrations can lead us to freedom.

A wild horse trapped in a pen paces around and around inside its prison, studying the situation. Eventually it walks to the center of the enclosure, tosses its head in the air, and gallops toward the fence. With a graceful leap it clears the barrier and regains its freedom.

~ *Recall a life-frustration.*
~ *Has it occurred repeatedly?*
~ *Begin a process of self-examination.*
~ *Ask God to help you know yourself better.*
~ *Pray for those who frustrate you and are frustrated.*

GENEROSITY

You will be enriched in every way
for your great generosity.
2 Corinthians 9:11

Generosity is often associated with charity, such as feeding the hungry and relieving the poor, supporting movements for justice and peace, and, more recently, repairing and preserving the natural environment. Closer to home, generosity is directed toward family, friends, and colleagues. But more intimately, we can be generous to ourselves.

Generosity toward ourselves may seem self-indulgent—surely we should think of others before ourselves! But if we are to be good custodians of the gift of life given to us, we need to honor it generously, so that it, in turn, can nourish generously the gift of life in others. This means honoring our bodies, honing our minds, and tending our emotions—becoming as balanced and whole as possible—so that we can fulfill our humanity and be a blessing in the world.

If we have received little of this world's goods, we may despair of being very generous to others. But we do have invaluable gifts to offer—our compassion, our kindness, our prayer. Generosity through prayer is a powerful way of serving. The host of people who suffer, the world of nature in travail—we can hold them in our hearts with sincere constructive intention. By reminding ourselves to do this frequently, we can make our life a generous prayer.

The generosity of life is matchless. The universe teams with awareness and energy, each sentient entity sharing God's gift of life. Joining this generous symphony, giving of ourselves to the life of the universe, is wonderfully life-giving in turn.

~ In what ways have others been generous to you?
~ In what ways could you be generous to others?
~ In what ways could you be generous to you?
~ Ask God for help in being generous.
~ Pray for an increase of generosity.

GENTLENESS

Show by your good life
that your works are done with gentleness born of wisdom.
James 3:13

Our world is often a harsh, not gentle, place. Business is competitive. Personal life is often turbulent. Even recreation can be stressful. As a result, we can become increasingly defensive and develop habitual means to protect ourselves. We tend to grow thick skins.

Unfortunately, a thick skin not only protects us from experiencing harshness, but also inhibits us from expressing gentleness. It takes a fierce energy to penetrate such resistance, whether the energy is coming in or going out. As a result, we may deaden our ability to feel both pain and pleasure.

Harsh methods may achieve quick results, but they often spawn fear and resentment. The gentle approach, although perhaps slower, nurtures creativity and growth. A gentle reprimand or encouragement demonstrates respect for the humanity of other people. Gentleness honors their dignity and allows their will to express freely. And it encourages reciprocal respect, so that we, in turn, are more likely to be treated with gentleness.

Similarly, if we are gentle with ourselves, forgiving errors in judgment and allowing time for growth, we give ourselves the opportunity to develop confidence and composure, instead of confusion and anxiety—an effective formula to negotiate the challenges of life.

A fierce rain beats down ferns and flowers, damaging as it nourishes. After a soft rain, the fronds stand tall and the blossoms spread their fragrance. A rough sea sends waterbirds to shore. On a calm sea, the birds swim and forage with ease. Gentleness nurtures life.

~ *Has the gentleness of someone else helped you?*
~ *Has your gentleness to yourself helped you?*
~ *How could your gentleness help others?*
~ *Ask God to let you know gentleness.*
~ *Pray for a world of gentleness.*

GLADNESS

You have put gladness in my heart
more than when . . . grain and wine abound.
Psalm 4:7

Gladness is a notoriously elusive emotion. The more we seek it, the more it eludes our grasp. We may strive to attain gladness by acquiring things, experiences, even people. But when we have them, we may not enjoy the reward we had expected. So we strive even more.

True gladness does not result from possessing things or people, of course, but from opening our hearts and giving our love to them, by appreciating the way they grow and mature or serve and honor all life— friends and families, vocations and recreations; lakes and rivers, trees and flowers, mountains and prairies.

As well as opening our hearts, we need to use our minds and exercise discernment in order to protect ourselves from depletion or abuse by unworthy influences and involvements. But when the recipient is worthy and our giving is free, the gladness is great. When we give ourselves, the richness of the universe flows to us, and through us. We experience the love and gratitude of other living entities, the splendor and magnificence of nature, the grace and glory of God.

Gladness brings us closer to the peace and joy of the divine spirit, closer to our own original and potential blessedness in the heart of God. Through the rich interconnectedness of existence, our gladness increases the gladness of all creation.

Water bubbles from a rock fissure, high in the mountains. It chuckles over pebbles and crevices, soon to join other streams. It splashes through a gully, and pours gleefully down a slope. Now rushing and curling over the lip of a precipice, it plummets laughing into the vortex below.

~ *Can you open your heart to someone or something?*
~ *Let the energy of gladness flow into your heart.*
~ *Thank God for your portion of the divine spirit.*
~ *Consider someone who is without gladness.*
~ *Pray that the person may know gladness.*

GRACIOUSNESS

Those who love a pure heart and are gracious in speech
will have the king as a friend.
Proverbs 22:11

The word *gratis* means "free, freely given, no strings attached." Graciousness, a derivative of *gratis,* suggests sensitive giving. The gift is not foisted on the recipient. There is no attempt to impress or overwhelm, to inflict guilt or exact payment. Instead, there is consideration for the independence and judgment of the recipient, openness to the feelings and desires of the other. And there is an implicit trust in whatever gifts the other may possess.

A gracious host offers hospitality, without obliging guests to reciprocate. A gracious employer provides organizational structure, letting workers exercise their skills. A gracious parent provides responsible support, allowing children to err and learn.

When, through gracious giving, we show appreciation for the gifts and abilities of another, we extend the gift of freedom for the other to develop, and to become, in turn, a sensitive giver. Free from the strictures of expectation or demand, the recipient is at liberty to enjoy the gift and honor the giver, by following the example.

But what of those who, granted a gracious gift, misuse the trust invested in them? They may find themselves recipients less often. Those who violate the gift, and consequently demean the giver, may look in vain for a repetition of the favor.

We stand on a high promontory overlooking a broad landscape. Below us spread the hills and valleys, the lakes and rivers—each geological feature supporting the others, yet performing its own function. There is both individual and blended beauty. A gracious scene.

~ *Do you know any particularly gracious people?*
~ *What qualities distinguish them as gracious?*
~ *How could you be more gracious to others?*
~ *Consider gifts that would be appropriate.*
~ *Pray for an increase of graciousness.*

_____

_____

_____

_____

_____

_____

_____

_____

_____

_____

_____

_____

_____

_____

_____

GRATITUDE

Let the peace of Christ rule in your hearts . . .
And be thankful.
Colossians 3:15

Gratitude tends to be a rare feeling these days, especially in our culture, where satisfaction is associated with the acquisition of physical pleasures and material things. There is always more to acquire! Our gratitude is frequently tinged with regret that the success or reward was not greater. This feeling of never being satisfied can leech the joy out of life. How can it be remedied?

If we could see our goal as a light to illumine our path, instead of a ruler to measure our success, then the very process of traveling toward the goal might offer us enjoyment on the journey. We could gain satisfaction from our experience on the way, as well as our achievement on arrival.

But focusing our attention on the daily process can be difficult, especially in a world where we feel pressured to race ahead to the next task. If, instead, we could occasionally recall those things in a day, week, month, or year for which we can be grateful, then we might be surprised by gratitude.

What has lifted our hearts? Who has given us happiness? How has creation raised our spirits? If we could take a few minutes to note those things that bring us gratitude, we might need more paper than we think! As we gradually grow in gratitude, we may find more things to be grateful for.

When winter storms pile up the snow and gray cold lingers in the North, people often wonder if relief will ever come. But then in spring, the mounds of snow melt down into the soil and run off over the waterways, providing needed moisture to green the grateful earth.

~ List the things and events you are grateful for.
~ List the people you are grateful for.
~ Does being grateful change your outlook?
~ Thank God for your good fortune.
~ Pray for more gratitude in the world.

GRIEF

You note trouble and grief,
that you may take it into your hands.
Psalm 10:14

Things or people or experiences that we cherish become part of us. If we lose them, we lose part of ourselves. When this happens, we need to recollect ourselves, that is, to remember our self-identity and purpose in life. Then we will not be permanently torn apart, unable to act and grow as whole people.

Initially we may feel broken, angry, and alone. It is absolutely necessary to respect and respond to our feelings. If we fail to honor our emotions, they may possess us, and then we, too, can be lost.

Grief can be complicated by guilt from a past mistake. But in time we may learn from our error and be better able to let it go. We may feel regret for the anguish a person endured before death, or for an apparently unfulfilled life. But a departed person is beyond our regret. For all we know, their deepest life purpose may have been achieved.

We do not have to face the challenge of grief alone. We can find comfort and support with people, animals, nature, and God's spirit. In the wisdom and beauty of nature, in the voices and arms of friends, God is strongly present. Grateful for all that we have learned from the loss, we can resume our life identity and purpose, perhaps with sadness but surely with wisdom.

The sea changes always. Now calm, now turbulent. The rollers surge and foam in endless pattern. The clouds cast fleeting shadows on the waves. The sun ignites the crests with glittering gold. All is vitality and movement—and continual change.

~ *Have you ever lost a part of yourself in grief?*
~ *How were your identity and life purpose changed?*
~ *Recall the things that brought you comfort.*
~ *Offer a prayer for a friend who has known loss.*
~ *How could you offer support to a person in grief?*

_____

_____

_____

_____

_____

_____

_____

_____

_____

_____

_____

_____

_____

_____

_____

_____

GUILT

Then I acknowledged my sin to you, . . .
and you forgave the guilt of my sin.
Psalm 32:5

Guilt can be a motivator, prompting us to repair the damage we may have done. It can also be a driver, forcing us into frenetic activity to mask our feelings and to bolster our self-esteem. In order not to be disabled by guilt, we need to acknowledge it and discover the reasons for it. Once the causes are known, we can take steps to respond constructively, and move toward reparation and restoration.

When someone says or suggests that we have done wrong, we need to consider the situation. Are they trying to control us—either intentionally or unconsciously? If so, we may be justified in feeling sympathy, but not guilt. Are they truly hurt? If so, we have compromised not only their well-being, but our sense of right—our conscience.

Conscience is an expression of the Divine within us. If our conscience is offended, then we have, to some extent, separated ourselves from God. When we consider that God is both inside and outside us—deeper and farther than we can imagine—then guilt is a signal that we have become disconnected not only from others, but from our true selves and the universe.

By contrast, forgiveness allows us to reconnect with the Divine. When we forgive and are forgiven, our guilt is resolved and separation is reconciled. We again unite with all life. We become whole.

During autumn, each hemisphere of the earth tilts away from the central sun. As the light weakens, life retreats. The weather turns cold. The leaves fall and the grass withers. But during spring, each hemisphere tilts toward the sun. As the light strengthens, life returns. And all nature luxuriates.

~ *Do you feel guilt for having offended someone?*
~ *Do you feel guilt for having offended yourself?*
~ *Ask God to help you find forgiveness.*
~ *Ask God to help you forgive others.*
~ *Pray for someone disabled by guilt.*

HAPPINESS

Emotions provide the motivating power in our lives. Yet Western culture tends to regard strong emotional expression as weakness. We especially feel compelled to conceal negative emotion, such as worry, grief, or fear. But we tend to glorify happiness, and even commercially promote it.

Normally it is healthy to express our feelings constructively, providing that we harm no one, of course. But there is perhaps one instance when we can benefit, at least temporarily, by reserving emotional expression.

We may have a long-term goal, a project that will promote our happiness. We feel good about it, and we want to share it. But to benefit from our enthusiasm, we need to conserve the emotional energy. We can reveal our plans to those who will support us concretely or emotionally, but we can also keep the extra energy to ourselves. Then we will empower our present efforts and increase the potential for our future happiness.

Happiness is infectious. Whether or not we express it, our whole being exudes it. We become a center of positive energy, radiating confidence and enthusiasm, attracting and inspiring others. We form a channel on earth for the joy of the spirit.

As her time to give birth approaches, a female fox searches for a secluded spot. Behind a tangle of leaves and branches, or under a fallen log or boulder, she digs a hidden den. Many dangers will threaten her young kits. But there in the darkness, secret and safe, she will join in the mystery of creation and know happiness.

~ *Consider some emotions that you feel you should not show.*
~ *How could you transform and express them constructively?*
~ *Consider a goal that would benefit from conserved energy.*
~ *Who would share your enthusiasm and support you?*
~ *Offer a prayer for people without goals or happiness.*

HATE

Let love be genuine; hate what is evil,
hold fast to what is good.
Romans 12:9

People who suffer severe injustice often respond with hate. They want to fight back. But responding to injury with injury only magnifies hate. Entrenched hatred is the most vicious problem on earth, corrupting souls and inflicting pain on billions near and far. What then can we do?

First, we can raise our spiritual shield. We can ask God to protect and guide us. We can fortify ourselves by realizing that we are in the divine presence, wherever we are, whatever we do. We can also examine ourselves, perhaps with the help of prayer and a journal, or a friend and counselor. We may find that the hate we feel is really a projection onto others, or the world, of something in us that we do not acknowledge.

Second, if the hatred is indeed outside us, we can work to change it. We can try to understand the position of the other side. Why did they direct their hatred toward us? What do they think and feel? How might we have contributed to these feelings? Where can we find ground for dialogue? It is possible that those who do ill are pursuing what they consider good. We might try to help them understand the destructive results of their actions, even for their own souls. Sometimes our enemies are our greatest teachers.

A forest fire is terrible. Trees and grasses explode in flames. Animals flee in reckless terror. But eventually, frustrated perhaps by cooling waters, the conflagration dies. And over time, the trees and animals return. Destruction precedes regeneration.

~ *Think of something you find particularly hateful.*
~ *Is it truly outside you, or projected from within you?*
~ *Ask God to help you transform the hatred.*
~ *Pray that those who hate may come to love.*
~ *Pray for those who suffer another's hate.*

HOPE

*You are the hope of all the ends of the earth
and of the farthest seas.
Psalm 65:5*

Hope is often experienced as a wish, perhaps with little expectation of fulfillment. We may feel that, if we put too much energy into hope, we set ourselves up for disappointment. But the divine Creator has given us the gift of life, and the grace to create in our human way. It is up to us to honor that gift, to take responsibility for our future, and to aspire with hope.

There are a number of steps we might follow. We can identify a goal that is worthy and hurts no one. Describe in detail the goal and the stages toward it, either in writing or drawing. Hold the goal repeatedly in our mind's eye, imagining how it would feel to pursue and achieve it. And—most essential—place our hope in the hands of the divine Power that creates and sustains all life. Jesus said, "Whatever you ask for in prayer with faith, you will receive" (Matthew 21:22).

Such active and trustful prayer allows purpose and direction to enter our life. It can give us confidence in our ability to plan and shape our future. It can also place us in greater communication with the source of all our hope. Our goal may not be fulfilled in the way or time that we expect. But as we draw closer to the Highest Good, seeking divine guidance and involvement, we know that the best will be achieved.

A songbird feels the cold days and the long nights approaching. But she does not wait to starve or freeze in the dark. Yearning for warmth and light, she joins the flock and heads south. What inviting image guides her purpose? What untiring effort feeds her hope? What divine energy guides her flight?

~ *What goal do you earnestly hope for?*
~ *Consider whether your goal is worthy.*
~ *Define your goal and the way toward it.*
~ *Place yourself and your goal in divine hands.*
~ *Picture and feel yourself pursuing and achieving it.*

HUMILITY

When pride comes, then comes disgrace;
but wisdom is with the humble.
Proverbs 11:2

When people have gained a measure of success and mastery, they inspire our admiration and maybe also our fear. But when successful people demonstrate humility, they win our esteem.

False humility serves to protect us and control others. We may play humble to gain support or disarm aggressiveness. True humility recognizes our gifts and the gifts of others. Realistic in the knowledge of our own worth, we give others space to develop their gifts and welcome their talents and successes. Then they are more likely to appreciate our successes and may even offer their willing collaboration.

When we strive to develop true humility, we come to see ourselves more clearly and may discover character traits we wish to modify. Honesty and perseverance are needed for the work of inner change. It is easier to build walls around the old than to break new ground!

By allowing ourselves to grow, we tend to encourage growth in others and attract supportive associates and friends. We follow in the footsteps of Jesus, the Christ, who offered his life to enrich the lives of others and won the esteem of the world.

A single trout lily flowering on a spring hillside can easily be missed. The flower hangs down, and its face is hidden. If we stoop and gently turn the blossom to the sun, its exquisite beauty shines out. But when we stand back and gaze at the entire display, we are amazed by a splendor of yellow gold, hundreds of individual flowering gems, each lending its light to another.

~ *Consider the kind of humility you show.*
~ *Think of reasons for the esteem you deserve.*
~ *Pray for someone who lacks true humility.*
~ *Ask God to let you know true humility.*
~ *Consider giving someone space to grow.*

JOY

You show me the path of life.
In your presence there is fullness of joy.
Psalm 16:11

Joy is often mistaken for joviality, happiness, gladness, fun. Although these emotions may contribute to joy, the emotion mentioned in this quotation includes and surpasses all others, for it is the quintessence of pleasure, the participation in the divine presence.

The joy of the presence of God seems an experience beyond the reach of ordinary mortals, an elevated state reserved for mystics of the highest order. But if God is all powerful, all knowing, and in all places, there is no way that we can avoid the divine presence. We need only to become aware of it and sensitive to it.

How can we realize the presence of God? Many answers to this question have been suggested down the ages. One method is easily available to us. Instead of seeking the most exalted experiences, we can turn to the simplest and most basic. We can recall those moments that have brought a subtle flowering of joy in the soul. The glance of an eye, the sight of a landscape. The touch of a hand, the caress of a breeze. The timbre of a voice, the music of a waterfall.

We can let our memory of these special moments gather gently within us, until we feel an appreciation, a warmth, a joy rising from the deepest core of our being. Then we know that we are resting in the power and presence of God.

We pause in the cathedral of nature. By a forest stream gurgling over pebbles and rocks—the sound lifts our feelings. On a mountain precipice overlooking vast snow peaks—the wind clears our thoughts. In a leafy wood filtering the sunlight and shadows—the stillness soothes our spirit.

~ *Recall a moment of simple but profound joy.*
~ *Dwell on the feeling and let it grow in your soul.*
~ *Thank God for opening divine presence to you.*
~ *Offer a moment of joy to someone you know.*
~ *Pray that they may know the presence of God.*

KINDNESS

Whoever pursues righteousness and kindness
will find life and honor.
Proverbs 21:21

True kindness desires the very best for people. It sets an outstanding example in all avenues of life—relationships, career, recreation. But true kindness knows that people do their best and enjoy life most when they are at liberty to develop and follow their own paths. It also cautions or corrects people when they might take a wrong turn or possibly hurt themselves and others.

God gave us the gift of life and lets us live it freely. Cornering our affection or curbing our behavior might have kept us in check and saved us from knocks, but it might not have won our love or helped us grow. The joy that comes from nurturing maturity and fulfillment in another person, perhaps receiving their thanks and love, surpasses any reward to be gained from possessing or directing them.

A worthy example, generous support, and careful correction all express true kindness. Those who receive such a gift will surely pass it on. As a result, kindness will grow from soul to soul, from race to race, and from continent to continent. Our lives and the lives of others will be enriched by a flowering of kindness in the world.

A mother raccoon offers her young ones an example. They see her searching for food and fending off danger. But she gives them freedom to discover life for themselves, poking under rocks and roots, playing and scrapping with each other. At the first sign of danger, she growls fiercely, sending them under cover or up a tree. Their feelings may be hurt for the moment, but their skins will be saved.

~ *Do you know someone who shows true kindness?*
~ *Do you know someone who needs true kindness?*
~ *Consider how you could show kindness to this person.*
~ *What activities would help spread kindness in the world?*
~ *Ask God to help you be an example of true kindness.*

LONGING

O Lord, all my longing is known to you;
my sighing is not hidden from you.
Psalm 38:9

Longing is the result of deep emotional need. It often expresses as the desire to be with, to possess, or to merge with someone or something, or to achieve some goal. Longing in a conscious being may be compared to the laws of attraction in the physical world—gravity, electromagnetism, the strong and weak nuclear forces. Although attractive forces manifest in different ways, they appear to operate in all forms of existence and levels of consciousness.

Our longing for the treasures of earth and the riches of relationship is but a poignant melody in the symphony of longing for the Divine Source of all attraction. So longing is not a negative feeling to be ignored and suppressed. If we ignore our longings, we deny our natural urge to participate in the operation of the universe and to discover our true home. In effect, we stifle the life force within us.

Yet sometimes we cannot pursue our longings, as they may offend or injure someone else. In such cases, we may ask God to guide our wills and purify our longings. But it is profoundly stimulating to experience longing, even unfulfilled. When we do so, we become more fully alive, more completely involved in the attracting love that binds all things, and all souls, in one.

The particles of the atom and molecules of matter, the planets of the solar system and stars of the galaxy, the members of a family and mates of the soul, associations for pleasure and organizations of business—all are brought together by the universal forces of attraction. And the universe is held together by the love of God.

~ *For what or whom are your longings?*
~ *Feel a longing without the fulfillment.*
~ *Remember a longing that has been fulfilled.*
~ *Empathize with the longing in another being.*
~ *Ask God to purify all longings in the world.*

LOVE

Above all, clothe yourselves with love,
which binds everything together in perfect harmony.
Colossians 3:14

The Old Testament books of the Bible speak of the physical consummation of love as "knowing." Often we associate love with passion and ecstasy, or perhaps even frustration and anguish, but we seldom think of it in terms of knowing or awareness. Perhaps if we pursued this ancient understanding, we might experience more joy and less pain in love.

In what ways can we expand our awareness of whom or what we love? There are at least two fundamental ways of knowing—exterior and interior, analysis and impression, thinking or feeling, left brain or right brain. Most often we know plenty of exterior realities—physical features, historical background, expressed needs. But we are less aware of the interior realities.

How can we acquire such knowledge? As well as using our five outer senses, we can engage our inner senses. This involves patient reflection and appreciation—the gentle holding of a person or object in our mind and heart, an open acceptance of received impressions and insights. Such intuitive inquiry can greatly enrich our knowledge and, not infrequently, our love.

If we gain a deeper knowledge of whom or what we love, our turbulent emotions can be less difficult to navigate and, therefore, less painful to endure. When we understand another point of view, our own situation looms not so large.

Try an experiment. In mind or body, visit a loved scene of natural beauty. Rest quietly in that place. Let yourself be wholly there. Sense the woven details of form and color. Feel the glowing essence of its soul. Let yourself unite with the focus of your love.

~ *Consider someone or something you love.*
~ *How well do you really know them?*
~ *How could you enhance your knowledge?*
~ *How well do you feel you know God?*
~ *How could you enhance your knowledge?*

_____

_____

_____

_____

_____

_____

_____

_____

_____

_____

_____

_____

_____

_____

LUST

You may escape . . . lust,
and may become participants of the divine nature.
2 Peter 1:4

Lust is an expression of raw energy. When it manifests, an instinctual longing rises within us, and we are drawn, almost irresistibly, toward the source of our desire. We are responding to a deep natural urge, and we feel intensely alive.

If we accept the teaching that all life is one and that all people share a spiritual connection—as children of the one Creator—then lust can be understood as an attempt to remedy our physical separation. But unless mutual attraction is felt, lust is normally destructive, compromising the integrity and autonomy of those involved. The desired one becomes a victim of another's aggression, and the desiring one becomes a victim of his or her own passion. Separation often results.

How can we avoid the adverse effects of lust? We might seek to express our instinctual energy constructively. Instead of trying to take what we want, we might resolve to give what we can—some personal expression of kindness, some public act of charity. By helping others through giving ourselves and our gifts to the world, we can enhance the solidarity—the oneness—of creation. Our energy will contribute not to separation but to wholeness, and lust will have flowered into love.

A snake embodies raw instinctual energy. Deft and sometimes deadly, a snake is also vital and beautiful. In the Judeo-Christian tradition, the serpent in the Garden of Eden symbolizes separation. On the emblem of healers—the caduceus—the serpents symbolize wholeness.

~ *Bring to mind a source of lust.*
~ *Is the strong desire mutually shared?*
~ *How could this energy express itself in giving?*
~ *How does the intention to give influence your desire?*
~ *Pray for someone or some group misguided by lust.*

MEANNESS

Those who are kind reward themselves,
but the cruel do themselves harm.
Proverbs 11:17

Petty cruelty and cheapness are two different vices with a similar purpose. Both serve to diminish the pleasure or welfare of someone, and usually to enhance the position and self-image of someone else. Normally the hurt seems trivial, neither remarkable nor even blameworthy. But when repeated, it can become seriously detrimental to emotional and material stability.

At one time, a person had little recourse against intimidating meanness. But increasingly, governments are legislating against physical and emotional abuse in places of work and recreation and in the home. Those who find themselves victims now have recourse to counseling, support, and reparation.

The best way to resist the insidious damage of repeated meanness is to identify weakness in the perpetrator and strength in the victim. What insufficiencies does the perpetrator experience, and how could they legitimately be remedied? What resources does the victim possess, and how could they charitably be employed? It may be possible for the victim, with personal advice and spiritual support, calmly and rationally to engage the challenge. Or it may be necessary, finally, to escape the threat of persistent pathology.

We have all heard stories of animal aggressiveness, particularly between males during the mating season. Rivals engage in ritual combat. But rarely does injury, or even death, result. More often, after they have adequately assessed their comparative stature and integrity, the combatants separate. The conflict ends. The animals preserve their self-respect—and their lives.

~ *Have you met meanness in yourself or another?*
~ *Discern the weakness in the perpetrator.*
~ *Discern the strength in the victim.*
~ *Pray that God may help both.*
~ *Pray for those in unequal contests.*

_____

_____

_____

_____

_____

_____

_____

_____

_____

_____

_____

_____

_____

_____

PAIN

You will have pain,
but your pain will turn into joy.
John 16.20

Pain is endemic to the human situation. All sentient life knows suffering, at least to the degree that it possesses consciousness and the ability to experience feeling. Science has devised countless well-known treatments to restore and maintain human health.

Pain may be an indication that something is harming us. Perhaps we frequent unsafe environments, eat unhealthy food, or think unpleasant thoughts. Pain is a signal that the operation of our body or soul has been damaged and thrown out of balance. How can we restore equilibrium?

Perhaps we could try to discern what pain is telling us about ourselves, how and where it afflicts us. We could then, without reproach, arouse our most sincere sympathy for ourselves, and give our deepest love to the afflicted part. And we could ask God to help us, to send us healing and wholesome energy.

We could also consider the pain of others, those even less fortunate than ourselves. We hear continually of hunger and poverty, sickness and disaster. We could think, with compassion, of people experiencing trouble similar to our own, and give them our sympathy and love. And we could ask God to send healing and reconciliation to a suffering world.

If prolonged hunger afflicts animals, their bodies sicken and die. If severe drought stresses trees, their leaves wither and fall. If fields and forests are ravaged or air and water are polluted, their life-giving power declines. The entire world needs love and healing.

~ *Ask God for healing and wholeness.*
~ *Send love and sympathy to your pain.*
~ *Consider the pain of other people.*
~ *Consider the pain of nature.*
~ *Pray for world healing.*

PATIENCE

Better is the end of a thing than its beginning;
the patient in spirit are better than the proud in spirit.
Ecclesiastes 7:8

Does it seem strange to call patience an emotion? Patience can certainly be invaluable in managing emotion—not by giving us more time to suppress feeling, but by helping us to focus feeling constructively. Patience is beneficial in at least two different kinds of circumstances—when reacting to an emotionally charged situation or when planning to achieve an exciting goal.

By being patient, we give ourselves time to act more appropriately and effectively in most situations. We also provide ourselves an opportunity to savor the situation and our feelings about it. Even if the experience is difficult for us, the more we become aware of the circumstance and our own emotions, the more likely we are to respond in a way that is best for ourselves and others. We will possess greater awareness of our motives, and greater confidence in our actions.

Exercising patience in this way can allow us greater potential satisfaction not only in the outcome, but also in the process of working toward the outcome. As we arrest inappropriate reactions, analyze the situation, and plan our responses, we gain control of both ourselves and the situation. We boost our confidence, self-esteem, and pleasure. And we gain an innate sense of participating in the timeless operation of the universe.

Over millions of years, tectonic plates have ground together, raising vast folds of earth and jagged pinnacles of rock. Over hundreds of years, coniferous trees have clothed the valleys and alpine flowers have decorated the peaks. Mountains—the magnificent works of time.

~ *Recall a time of impatience.*
~ *What were your feelings?*
~ *What were the circumstances?*
~ *How could patience have helped?*
~ *Pray for more patience in the world.*

_____

_____

_____

_____

_____

_____

_____

_____

_____

_____

_____

_____

_____

_____

_____

PEACE

Peace I leave with you; my peace I give to you. . . .
Do not let your hearts be troubled, and do not let them be afraid.
John 14:27

How can we find peace? We can retreat from the responsibilities of life and turn inward to find the center of our soul. But when we arrive at the center, we may discover that our minds will not stop. Thoughts and feelings continually race through our brains. We can escape by traveling to the corners of the earth. No sooner do we reach our paradise destination, than we begin to look for diversions—interesting things or people—to occupy our attention.

Perhaps we have been searching for a false peace that we really do not want and cannot find. Instead of retreating inward or escaping outward, we may discover a measure of peace by balancing these divergent "directions." Peace for us may result not from shuttling between inner and outer, but from finding equilibrium among all the various aspects of our lives.

To find such balance, we need to engage more fully with life. When we care for ourselves, others, and the natural world, we begin to engage with all the different aspects of life. We cease to be torn in any one direction and begin to find a measure of balance. Strangely, we may discover that peace exists not in relinquishing ties, but in developing links with the marvelous life that exists all around and within us.

Our body knows peace when it is adequately fed, exercised, and rested. The same applies to our emotions, thoughts, and spirits. Our friends and associates know peace when they are served and honored. And the natural world finds equilibrium when it is conserved and respected.

~ *How do you find peace?*
~ *What do you try to avoid?*
~ *How could you find balance?*
~ *Consider someone needing peace.*
~ *Pray for all people who need peace.*

_____

_____

_____

_____

_____

_____

_____

_____

_____

_____

_____

_____

_____

_____

_____

_____

PRIDE

A person's pride will bring humiliation,
but one who is lowly in spirit will obtain honor.
Proverbs 29:23

Pride is closely related to self-esteem. But often the outer image, and not the inner identity, becomes the foundation of our pride.

A consumer-oriented culture persuades us to measure ourselves against models that inadequately complement our true identity. We are bombarded with advertising that pressures us to acquire goods and pursue activities apparently essential for our happiness. But they often fail to satisfy.

We are encouraged to compare ourselves with others, ranking them higher or lower than we are. But such comparisons are misguided. We are all on the path together, and only at different stages. All people are images of God, working toward fulfillment of the image. The fact that someone seems less favored than we are should elicit our support rather than our conceit.

How then could pride be a beneficial emotion, a constructive motivator? Here is a suggestion.

Perhaps when we freely serve and appreciate the created order—the life all around and within us—we may rightly be proud of our Creator and creation. Such pride would derive from our gratitude for inclusion in the divine plan, and from our companionship in the relatedness of all things. We would not draw hurtful comparisons, but instead know the thrill of contributing to the marvelous life of the universe.

At dawn and dusk, especially in spring, a walk by a marsh or wetland is a wonderful experience. The trees are exuberant with birdsongs, and the reeds with the trill of spring peepers. Is it possible that all are proud to be alive?

~ *Of what can you legitimately be proud?*
~ *How is this pride shared with others?*
~ *How is it shared with all creation?*
~ *Ask God to purify your pride.*
~ *Ask God to purify all pride.*

_____

_____

_____

_____

_____

_____

_____

_____

_____

_____

_____

_____

_____

_____

_____

_____

REGRET

The blessing of the LORD makes rich,
and he adds no sorrow with it.
Proverbs 10:22

Nothing is perfect in this life. Even when we succeed, there is often something we could have done better. And when in our own eyes we fail, the burden of regret can sometimes be overwhelming. Not only our ego may be damaged; our position in life may be impaired.

But we will not benefit from letting regret depress and debilitate us. Instead, we may learn and grow by analyzing past actions and determining the reasons for apparent mistakes. We may learn what extenuating circumstances pressed upon us or why certain decisions may have seemed right. We may find what factors of personality influenced our thinking, and how changing our approach might enhance future choices.

If we have hurt someone, we can attempt to repair the damage and make amends. If we have hurt ourselves, we can resolve to forgive our humanity and move forward with gratitude for lessons learned and maturity gained. As we forgive, so we will be forgiven. There are blessing and comfort in the words of this great law that Jesus taught us. We may have erred, but we have also graduated from one level of experience to another, and have advanced in the school of life.

The light of such hard-won understanding may help to restore our spirits, clarify our thinking, and increase our chances of future success. We may even discern unexpected benefits accruing from our apparent mistakes!

Sunset is both the ending of one day and the promise of another. The sun departs in glowing color, the sky darkens, the stars appear. We may feel nostalgia, maybe pleasure, perhaps regret. There is also the promise of a new day and a new light.

~ *Remember a choice that you regret.*
~ *What were the extenuating circumstances?*
~ *Consider any possible resulting benefits.*
~ *Determine the lessons you have learned.*
~ *Pray for assistance to make amends.*

_____

_____

_____

_____

_____

_____

_____

_____

_____

_____

_____

_____

_____

_____

_____

_____

RESPECT

Pay to all what is due them . . .
respect to whom respect is due.
Romans 13:7

The first chapter of the first book in the Old Testament describes in symbolic terms the creation of nature and humanity. We are told that God created the natural world in six days, and that every day God said it was good. And we are told that God made humanity in the image of God. We hear the message that all existence proceeds from God, is inherently sacred, and unequivocally deserves our respect.

But how do we regard those aspects of existence that seem furthest from any conception of the Divine? For example, what about the mean or base, the corrupt or violent? Do people who display these characteristics still possess the divine image? If the answer is yes, then at a certain level we need to respect them. They may be attempting to achieve what, in their current understanding, seems good to them.

When we respect all creation, we cannot ignore the existence of either good or evil. In some circumstances we may need to protect ourselves or assist others in order to avoid harm and promote healing. But if we appreciate the divine in ourselves and others, if we allow it to grow and flower, then we may find a way to mutual respect. We may perceive the good of each individual becoming the good of creation, the good of all.

A krummholz pine clings tenaciously to the rocky mountain slope. Bent by gale force winds and heavy snow, stunted by poor nourishment and the brief growing season, its battered beauty is a shelter to the golden-mantled ground squirrel who burrows beneath its roots, and a welcome sign of life and hope to the adventurous mountain hiker.

~ *Consider your personal characteristics.*
~ *What do you find difficult to respect?*
~ *Can you find basic goodness there?*
~ *Consider characteristics of others.*
~ *Look for basic goodness there.*

SADNESS

I will turn their mourning into joy . . .
and give them gladness for sorrow.
Jeremiah 31:13

Sadness grows from a sense of loss. If we allow ourselves to be trapped in sadness, it can sap our zest and skill for living. Moving beyond sadness requires support from the depth of our being, and from the Source of all being. To lift the weight of sadness we need great strength. How can this be done?

We might try to discern the cause of our sadness. Often sadness builds over time, like steam in a kettle, because we resist unpleasant memories, and try to "keep the lid on." By examining past feelings and carefully exposing ourselves to their memory and power, we can gently lift the lid, and slowly let the feelings steam off. But reliving difficult emotions takes courage. They can temporarily overwhelm us. We may want to involve a friend or counselor.

A general feeling of sadness also may indicate our sensitivity to a suffering world. If this is our experience, we can be grateful that our connection with the universe is expanding, and that our capacity to respond may consequently grow. By touching this universal sadness, we become aware of life's harsh realities. But we also touch a deeper purpose—a sense of the wholeness God intends.

When we observe a beautiful scene, we sometimes experience a gentle sadness. We may feel at one with the scene, yet strangely separate from it. We see a tiny bird, a single flower, a lone tree. Does sadness touch them? Would sadness derive from their seeming separation from the divine Source? Would this sadness also assure them of their ultimate connection with that Source? Blissful sadness!

~ *Discern a cause for sadness in the world.*
~ *Examine your feeling about this cause.*
~ *What response might be suitable?*
~ *Ask God to release you from sadness.*
~ *Pray for people who experience sadness.*

SCORN

Blessed are you when people revile you . . .
for your reward is great.
Matthew 5:11-12

Scorn can lead to all manner of prejudice and evil, such as bullying, sexual harassment, racial discrimination, or even spoliation of the natural environment.

We find it difficult to accept people who exhibit traits that we cannot accept within ourselves. We often unconsciously project these unacceptable characteristics onto other people. If we notice ourselves being scornful, this may be a signal, prompting us to look critically at ourselves, to see if we can detect the unwanted trait within.

If we become the object of another's scorn, our feelings may be hurt. Even subtle slights, when repeated, can cause tremendous pain. We can remind ourselves that the scorner may be voicing an unconscious lack of self-acceptance. We can also remember that, as limited or mistaken as we may be, we are made in the image of God, and we join in the goodness of creation.

Each one of us is a unique creation equipped with particular gifts to pursue our particular life purpose. Rather than diminish our self-esteem, the opinions of others can encourage us to discover and express the unique creation that we are, and the special contribution that we have to offer God, humanity, and the world.

Countless property-owners expend hours of labor to extirpate the humble dandelion from their lawns. The small plant is widely scorned. But a carpet of dandelions is a stunning sight. The diaphanous seed globes form exquisite geometrical structures. And the juice from the leaves offers a miracle of healing.

~ *What personality characteristics do you scorn?*
~ *Are these characteristics within you?*
~ *For what have you been scorned?*
~ *Recall and esteem your gifts.*
~ *Pray for clarity of vision.*

SHAME

Do not let me be put to shame,
O Lord, for I call on you.
Psalm 31:7

When we have behaved in a way that has hurt someone else, or our-selves, and that is unworthy of a human being, we can truly and jus-tifiably feel ashamed. But when others deprecate us because of some artificial social standard—because we are not rich or young, sporty or beautiful in their eyes—or to maintain power over us, then we have no cause to hold onto shame.

If we have truly hurt someone and let ourselves down, then we can attempt to repair the damage. We can apologize and offer to serve in some constructive way. We can reshape our values and behavior, so that we will be less likely to make the same mistake again.

If, however, the wounded refuse to forgive us and accept our repara-tions, or the powerful continue to censure and manipulate us unjustly, then we need to find ways to recover from unnecessary shame.

We can review our motives and actions to determine what went wrong or how we might change, and then imagine our modified behav-ior in a similar future encounter. This may give us sympathy for the other and confidence in ourselves. We can question the motives of our oppressors to understand them better, and voice our concerns to them (if we have the energy) or leave them alone (if the cost is too great). This may win us reparation from them or relief for us.

Standing by a steep waterfall. Seeing the turbulent cascade. Hearing the roar and echo. Feeling the spray on hair and hands and face. The rush-ing torrent releases contained energy; refreshes earth, air, and water. A draught of purity and power for the thirsty soul!

~ *Recall some debilitating shame.*
~ *What is truly your responsibility?*
~ *What is manipulation from others?*
~ *Seek forgiveness where appropriate.*
~ *Pray for cleansing and strength.*

SYMPATHY

Have unity of spirit, sympathy, love for one another,
a tender heart, and a humble mind.
1 Peter 3:8

Sympathy is the glue that holds the human family together and keeps us in a mutually supportive relationship with our environment. Without sympathy there is meager response to the neediness and suffering of other people, and there is little care for the creatures of nature or the elements that support life—air, earth, and water.

Strangely enough, when we respond to another's need—either a person, an animal, a plant, or even soil—we become somehow linked to the other; and the other, in turn, becomes a support for us. A relationship is formed.

In the case of a human or an animal, we are given the opportunity to express qualities that represent the best in humanity—love, service, care for another. In the case of elemental nature, we are enabled to exercise our responsibility as stewards, and may be rewarded by the perpetuation of conditions that support life—stable weather, thriving forests, wholesome air and water, productive fields and orchards.

We also need to exercise discernment when we extend sympathy, in case we are responding to people's selfish ends. Although we might want to assist them, we would not want to support anything unworthy. Meditation and self-examination can help us to test our motives and the motives of others, before we extend and involve ourselves in sympathy.

The sun shines brightly in a clear blue sky. Fleecy clouds sail lazily overhead. Our mood is cheerful. But now the sky darkens. Massive thunderclouds swiftly advance. Lightning cleaves the horizon. Rain pelts down. And our feelings change. We are in sympathy.

~ *Recall someone who needs sympathy.*
~ *How are you now linked together?*
~ *Recall a loved thing in nature.*
~ *How are you linked with it?*
~ *Pray for world sympathy.*

WORRY

*Cast all your anxiety on him,
because he cares for you.*
1 Peter 5:7

To worry is human. If we have no worries, we might lack motivation and become trapped in complacency. But if we wallow in worry, we can waste our time and dissipate our energy. By employing worry as an incentive, we can use energy wisely.

Worry can signal a problem that needs to be resolved. Perhaps we are avoiding an issue that we would rather forget. We need to determine the causes of our worry. Then we can begin to address them. Sometimes under scrutiny, the most intractable problems solve themselves. Previously hidden solutions arise.

Sometimes we find ourselves bogged down in a quagmire, and we need to persevere to reach firmer ground. Taking constructive thought and action, and seeking divine assistance, will help us to move forward. Sometimes we discover that the problem is longer term, and we will just have to live with it. Adapting our attitudes or habits can go a long way toward easing the worry, if we cannot change our circumstances.

By wrestling with worry instead of letting it conquer us, we enlist our own life energy. By opening ourselves and our situation to the presence of God, we engage the Source of all energy. Our worry then becomes our incentive, and our life can be transformed.

When a wolf is hungry, it spares no effort in the search for food. It may travel extreme distances; seek rare scents, sounds, or movements; delve deeply under trees and rocks. It may spend hours, even days, patiently waiting for a sign or persistently following a trail. The animal employs its life energy to secure its life.

~ *Recall a particularly debilitating worry.*
~ *Try to identify the causes of your worry.*
~ *What could you do to alleviate the worry?*
~ *Consider your worry in the presence of God.*
~ *Formulate a prayer for someone who worries.*

_____

_____

_____

_____

_____

_____

_____

_____

_____

_____

_____

_____

_____

_____

CONTINUING ON THE PATH

I hope you've enjoyed working with your emotions over the past weeks or months, as suggested in this book.

When you follow any discipline of self-exploration, you give yourself opportunity to learn more about yourself, other people, and the world around you. Not all you learn may be equally welcome, but most of it will be useful. As you work with the information you receive, you may find that your life and your environment become more to your liking. As a result, you will gain greater confidence and competence in living.

You may discover that you are able, to a surprising degree, to responsibly create your own life in cooperation with the Creator, and that, when you ask for divine guidance, you receive help, inspiring you to learn and grow, discover and fulfill your dreams.

Where will you go from here? By asking this question of yourself with God's help, you learn what is best and how to pursue it. As you know, when you appeal to divine guidance, the response is not always what you expect. An intuition, an event, or a person may lead you in a new way.

But when you approach the Highest Good, our Creator and Source, the response is ultimately best for you, others, and the world. You will be guided to ask questions, read resources, and meet people to help you in your quest. May you find true love and companionship, joy and fulfillment on your journey!